Banking on Stellar Service

Strategies to Ensure Your Financial Institution Stands Out

By Jim DeMaio

Revenant Publishing

Dear Bill
All the Best!
5-30-19

First published 2019 by Revenant Publishing

Printed in the United States of America

Library of Congress Cataloging-in-Publication Data
Banking on Stellar Service: Strategies to Ensure Your Financial Institution Stands Out / written by Jim DeMaio / edited by Cheryl Grayson / cover design and graphics by VisualArts / interior layout by Cindie Cagenello

ISBN: 978-0-578-45398-9 (pbk.: alk. Paper)
1. Business – Banking – Examples. 2. Finance – Banking – Examples. 3. Management – Customer Service – Examples. 4. Leadership – Supervision – Examples.

I. DeMaio, Jim, 1961 –

HA41-7358231911-dc22 2071054227 2042165338

Revenant Publishing strives to use environmentally responsible suppliers and materials to the fullest extent possible in the publishing of its books. Such materials include vegetable-based, low-VOC inks and acid-free papers that are recycled, totally chlorine-free, or partly composed of non-wood fibers. For more information, visit our website Revenant.Pub.

Paperback printing 10 9 8 7 6 5 4 3 2 1

Table of Contents

Acknowledgements

This book would not be possible without the extraordinary collaboration of all the banks and bankers I enjoyed working with throughout the past 20 years. The invaluable experience of coming alongside you and learning from you remains an honor and a pleasure as I look ahead to many more years of working together.

I hope this book serves you both as a reader and an active participant in implementing actionable changes that make your bank more customer-focused. To that point, you will notice each chapter concludes with "Questions for Reflection" and space for you to add your personalized notes. With your thoughts, you in effect become co-author of this copy of **Banking on Stellar Service**. Please drop me a note and let me know the additions you make here. I always welcome your comments and reflections as we continue our work together

I am grateful to work with an amazing group of colleagues at Learning Dynamics, our national talent management company. Your commitment to providing quality learning and development solutions for our clients is much appreciated. I especially thank my colleagues Barbara Phillips, Greg Slomba, and Mary Sue Cavanagh for your review of the drafts of this book.

Thanks also to our terrific Interns Natasha Tenreiro, Nicole Mowry, and Nate Keegan for your assistance with the book. And many thanks to my colleague, Cheryl Grayson, for creating the helpful illustrations featured throughout the book.

On a personal level, I must express my deepest gratitude to my wonderful wife, Debbie. I cannot thank you enough for your love and support over the past two decades.

Introduction

The banking industry is changing. Less foot traffic in branches and increased digitalization are just two of the significant changes banks face.

What hasn't changed is the ability to stand out from the competition by providing outstanding customer service. Banks who understand this reap the benefit of loyal, long-time customers. Banks that don't will be mired in mediocre performance, or fail.

Intended to provide the reader with practical tips, each chapter of this book addresses components of a service-oriented culture for banks. The chapters conclude with questions to reflect upon and consider for your financial institution.

The fact that you are reading this book suggests that you probably "get it" when it comes to customer service. In that case, my hope is that whether you are a bank president, a director of retail banking, or a branch manager, there will be nuggets you pick up that will enhance what you are already doing to maintain a customer-centric bank.

How To Get The Most from This Book

Structured to provide easily implemented approaches for improving and maintaining the excellence of your financial institution, simply using the table of contents may be sufficient for finding the information you seek. Additionally, every chapter follows this formula: What/ Why/How and Questions for Reflection to stimulate thinking and action.

Lastly, within each chapter you'll receive examples of best practices and not-so-best practices. These practices are highlighted by two bank icons: Better Bank and Blunder Bank. Meant to call attention to what's possible — the good, the bad, and the really bad — Better Bank and Blunder Bank will help illustrate how actual financial institutions have leveraged best practices or made missteps that limit their success. These icons are peppered throughout the book to help you quickly find such examples.

Chapter 1

"Hire for Attitude, Train for Skill"

It begins with the hiring process. Some banks get hung up on the amount of previous banking experience candidates have. While banking experience can be essential for higher level positions, for entry-level positions such as tellers (or Universal

Bankers), it can be beneficial to also seek those who have worked in retail or other settings where they have worked extensively with customers.

Ensure that those supervisors interviewing candidates use behavioral interview questions. The premise with these questions is that candidates' future behavior is best predicted by their past behavior. Ask behavioral interview questions, not fluff questions such as, "What are your strengths?," where savvy candidates will provide infomercial responses they believe the interviewer wants to hear.

Behavioral interview questions lessen the chance of candidates providing infomercial responses.

For Universal Bankers, or call center positions, where the employee will have direct customer contact, consider using the following behavioral interview questions to assess how service-oriented the person is.

- Tell me about a time when you worked with an angry customer and what you did to diffuse the anger.

- Give me an example of a time when you provided what you would consider "Wow" service.

- Tell me about a time when you had to resolve a customer problem that was caused by your company.

- How would you handle an unhappy customer who insists on seeing your manager?

Responses to the above questions will give you an indication as to how the person will respond when these situations arise at your financial institution.

The best responses to behavioral interview questions are specific and recent. Responses that are dated and too general may suggest that the candidate has little customer service experience with the situation you are asking about.

Also use behavioral interview questions with candidates for higher level positions such as branch managers, commercial lenders, and back office supervisors. It is critical that those vying for these roles be service-oriented, especially if they will have direct reports who they will be coaching to reinforce your service standards.

Be mindful that a positive, "can do" attitude shown by candidates usually translates into an employee who will provide stellar service. Those candidates who appear to have higher levels of emotional intelligence — especially relationship management and self-awareness — usually provide excellent service to customers. Conversely, candidates lacking in self-awareness, who don't realize they have an edge when working with customers, are not who you want working with your customers.

When hiring for a back office or support staff position, assess whether the person will provide stellar internal service to other employees. Having back office staff who do not provide good internal service will hurt those customer-facing employees.

It is not uncommon to hear about instances where the interviewer(s) did not ask specific behavioral interview questions, and then later was surprised when the person came aboard and did not demonstrate the customer service skills needed for the position. Other times, the interviewer does too much talking and does not learn enough about the candidate's customer service skills.

Blunder Bank

At Blunder Bank, when there are open positions, the interviewer(s) asks basic, non-specific questions about customer service. These supervisors also do too much talking, and don't learn about the candidates and how service-oriented they are. It should, therefore, not be surprising that the bank has many employees who do not provide stellar service. In fact, the bank's mystery shops often include examples where the shoppers rated the employees as mediocre or worse. The turnover at Blunder Bank is also significant, as employees hired do not always have a high level of internal, and/or external service, and end up leaving or being terminated.

Better Bank

At Better Bank, supervisors receive training on behavioral interviewing to ensure that they ask specific service-oriented questions of candidates. Hiring managers are also encouraged to consider candidates with non-banking service experience. Managers are also held accountable for their new hires, so that if management notices a high level of customer complaints or service problems with a particular branch or department, that branch or department's manager will be questioned to determine the root cause of the problem.

Coaching Tip

Sit in on part of an interview with hiring managers to see if they are asking behavioral interview questions. After the interview, provide the hiring manager with feedback to strengthen his or her skills.

Questions for Reflection

1. Are your bank's managers trained to ask behavioral interview questions?

2. Do your hiring managers consider how important a positive attitude is as it relates to stellar service?

3. Does your bank management speak with managers when they see patterns of poor service from new hires within those managers' branches or departments?

Notes

Chapter 2

Hold Managers Accountable for Stellar Service

The role of a bank manager in fostering a culture of service cannot be overestimated. After all, it is the manager who needs to coach employees to provide stellar internal and/or external service.

It is also the manager who must be held accountable

for his or her department or branch's service.

Senior managers need to take note of departments or branches with recurring service problems. Managers of these departments should be questioned about the service problems.

While it's one thing for a department or branch to have a service blip, it's another for the department or branch to have a pattern of service problems. Senior management should not put up with continuing service problems stemming from a particular department or branch.

Managers must understand that those whose staff continually struggle with customer service will likely have that reflected in their performance reviews. One would hope that the bank's performance appraisal system includes a competency regarding service.

Managers overseeing departments or branches with consistent service problems are likely not long for the bank.

We know of a bank where "Marsha" has been a long-time manager of a back office department. Marsha's knowledge of bank operations is outstanding. However,

Marsha believes that some of the branch staff overly rely on her staff to respond to customers' problems. She has fostered an adversarial relationship with the bank's Retail staff, which is conveyed to her own team, leading them to provide less than stellar internal service to the Retail staff. Unfortunately, this bank's senior management focuses on Marsha's outstanding knowledge of operations, and does not hold her accountable for her poor service to the Retail staff.

On the other hand, branches or departments who consistently provide stellar service almost always have a manager who holds his or her staff accountable for outstanding service. These managers provide coaching that reinforces good service or works to improve service problems.

Blunder Bank

At Blunder Bank, there are managers in both customer and non-customer facing areas where the service is spotty, at best. However, instead of holding these managers accountable, the bank has its head in the sand and hopes that the service will improve on its own. Instead, the service problems remain, adversely impacting both internal and external customers. The teamwork within these departments and branches also is lacking.

Better Bank

At Better Bank, when patterns of service problems are noticed, management takes action. They look for the source of the problem and work to rectify it. If a manager's team continually has service problems, that manager is given an opportunity to improve, and if no improvement is made, is managed out of the financial institution. Also, managers whose teams consistently demonstrate stellar service are recognized.

Coaching Tip

Work with managers who have more than their share of employees demonstrating poor service. Look to see how the manager can set a culture within his or her department or branch that reinforces the importance of stellar service.

Questions for Reflection

1. Are your managers held accountable for their staff providing stellar service?

2. Do you look for patterns of sub-par service within certain departments or branches?

3. Do you make the consequences clear to managers whose teams have consistent service problems?

Notes

Chapter 3

Remove "Fish that Stink from the Head"

As noted in the previous chapter, a bank may find that a certain department or branch is consistently embroiled with service problems.

Often, when that is the case, it is also determined that the department or branch's manager is not service-oriented. Since the team takes its cues from that manager, they often will mimic the service (or lack thereof) that they see their manager providing. For instance, if the staff sees that the manager dismisses customers and takes a long time to return phone calls, they may do the same.

Sometimes, managers whose teams have continual service problems have backgrounds where they have less direct experience as service providers. For example, these managers may be more compliance or operations-driven, and less customer-centric.

In order for a team's service to improve, it may be necessary to remove the manager who is not customer-centric, and replace him or her with someone who is. However, this should be a last resort. Put a plan in place by providing tools and suggestions on how the manager can become more customer-centric. If the manager still does not show improvement, then you may need to manage him or her out. Doing this sends a message to the team that the bank is serious about customer service. The employees will then understand the need to improve on the service provided, or also risk being separated from the bank.

Learning Dynamics worked with a bank whose vice

president of branch administration, "Jeff," was not very service-oriented. As a result, Jeff's staff was also not providing good service to the branches. The bank's new president noticed this and let Jeff know that his service needed to improve. The president sent Jeff to a training program on customer service and had Jeff shadow another VP who is service-oriented. After not seeing any progress, the president worked with Human Resources to manage Jeff out of the organization.

Blunder Bank

At Blunder Bank, there is a branch and back office department with histories of having service problems. In both cases, the managers of these areas are not known for providing quality service themselves.

However, because both managers have been with the bank for a long time, and also are well-liked by the bank's COO (who will also not win any customer service awards), nothing is done about their teams' consistent service problems. The reputation of both managers is widely known throughout the bank, and employees privately grumble about the poor service provided by both managers and their staff.

Better Bank

At Better Bank, if a certain department or branch has continuing service problems, senior management intervenes. It is then determined whether that manager's lack of service orientation is fixable. If not, the bank and the manager part company.

Coaching Tip

Providing specific metrics (e.g., shop scores) to a manager whose area is not providing quality service may help the individual understand the importance of customer service.

Questions for Reflection

1. Do you emphasize to managers the importance of fostering a service-oriented culture?

2. Have you given your managers the tools they need to consistently deliver great customer service?

3. When consistent service problems occur within a department or branch, do you assess whether the manager is at the root of the problem? Do you have the courage to part company with a long-time manager whose team is consistently having service problems?

Notes

Chapter 4

Hold Employees Accountable

Just as we discussed in Chapter 2 about bank managers being held accountable for stellar service, so too do bank employees need to be held accountable.

Reinforce your bank's service standards to ensure

that employees are providing quality service. Also use your mystery shop results in coaching discussions with your employees. (By the way, one sign that a financial institution is not service-centric is if they do not mystery shop their branches and call center.)

When employees provide stellar service, acknowledge this and provide them with positive feedback. When they consistently go above and beyond, look to recognize them.

At Lee Bank in Western Massachusetts, all employees are encouraged to perform "heroic acts" of service. This customer-centric culture permeates the bank. Their receptionist's title is "Director of First Impressions." A cross-functional committee at the bank compiles the heroic acts and recognizes the top ones. President Chuck Leach noted, "Our employees, both customer-facing and in the back office, know that in today's environment good service is needed to be competitive. We aim to take it up a notch by building customer intimacy that will result in long-term relationships and advocacy."[1]

---

1. Leach, Chuck. Telephone interview. 21 May 2018.

Some managers are conflict-averse and reluctant to speak with employees who are not providing good service. These managers hope that employees' service will improve when, in reality, it often does not. While many managers understandably do not relish having to provide negative feedback, it is important to do so when necessary.

Not holding a service-challenged employee accountable also has negative implications for the branch or department's morale and teamwork. Other employees see the poor service and may even have to clean up the service problems caused by the employee. Those other employees also lose credibility in their manager for not addressing the employee's service deficiencies.

A bank we work with has a branch that consistently has low shop scores. Two of the employees within that branch are known for "having an attitude," and this translates into poor service to customers. While others in the branch are aware of this, the branch manager has let this poor service continue. While she spoke with each employee about their need to provide better service, she has not followed up and held the employees accountable. Consequently, the morale in this branch suffers, as the manager has lost credibility with the rest of the team.

Managers should use the bank's performance management system to assess employees' levels of service. Those employees providing consistently stellar service should be recognized, and those who are not need to be coached.

With employees who are not providing quality service, managers can ask themselves whether employees can't or won't provide the quality service. If the problems stem from the employee struggling with a system to find and respond to customers with information, that may be a "can't" situation, where re-training or shadowing another employee will help. Conversely, if the employee generally has a negative attitude (Who hired them?!), this is likely a "won't" situation, which is tougher to turn around. In these instances, you may want to start progressive discipline consulting with Human Resources, and in accordance with the bank's policy.

Blunder Bank

At Blunder Bank, "Tina" is an employee in one of the branches. Tina has, unfortunately, developed a reputation as someone who is abrupt with both customers and co-workers. Tina's manager has reminded her entire staff of the importance of customer service, yet has not wanted to directly address Tina's service shortcomings. As a result, Tina continues to demonstrate poor service.

Better Bank

At Better Bank, "Consuelo" is an employee in one of the branches. Consuelo has started to develop a reputation as someone who can be abrupt with both customers and co-workers. Consuelo's manager has observed this behavior, documented it, and let Consuelo know that it will not be tolerated. The manager developed an action plan whereby she discussed with Consuelo the specific improvements needed. The manager recognized Consuelo when observing a positive behavior, and corrected an unacceptable behavior when observing that. Over the next few months, Consuelo's manager noticed a significant improvement in her service to customers and co-workers.

Coaching Tip

Sometimes an employee may lack the self-awareness about a behavior that goes against providing great service. Pointing this out to the employee may enable them to change the behavior.

Questions for Reflection

1. Do you recognize employees who consistently provide stellar service?

2. Do you confront employees who demonstrate poor internal or external service?

3. Do you use your financial institution's performance management system to assess the level of service your employees provide?

Notes

Chapter 5

Create a Service-Centric Culture

The adage of "take care of your employees and they will take care of customers" still rings true in the banking industry.

The "profitability arrow" on the following page shows this connection.

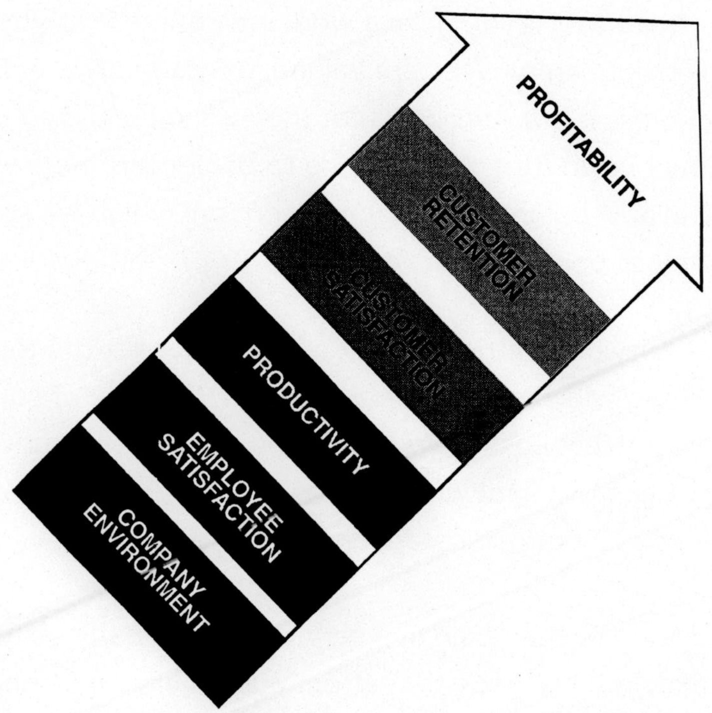

The above arrow is based, in part, on research conducted by Harvard some years ago. The Harvard researchers studied the Taco Bell organization and found that the most profitable Taco Bell stores had fewer employee relations issues and less turnover. Conversely, the least profitable Taco Bell stores had higher levels of those factors.[2]

---

2. Schlesinger, Leonard A., and James L. Heskett. "The Service-Driven Service Company" *Harvard Business Review*. September-October 1991. (1991): 2-20. Print.

Therefore, if you have a work environment at your bank where employees are valued, treated fairly, and respected, it is more likely that they will be satisfied and productive. In turn, their service to bank customers will be stellar, leading to customer retention, which we know is a key to bank profitability.

A service-centric banking culture starts at the top of the organization and cascades down. This type of culture reinforces that customers should be at the forefront of every decision. Bankwide service standards should be developed, communicated, and reinforced.

We know that even in a service-centric bank culture, mistakes will be made that affect customers. One senior vice president of retail banking learned that a long-time business customer was upset because he was charged an overdraft fee for his account being overdrawn by a couple of dollars. This progressive, customer-centric senior vice president had a plant sent to the business customer and included within it a roll of nickels and dimes. The note he wrote said, "We apologize and will be sure to waive your overdraft fee. We would never nickel and dime you."

The above story is an example of "service recovery." The way in which a bank responds to customers when there are service problems can actually strengthen the relationship between the customer and the bank. Yet, we sometimes see examples where bank employees, because they personally have not caused the customer problem, dig in their heels and will not even apologize to the customer.

Umpqua Bank, based in Portland, Oregon, is a great example of a financial institution with a service-centric culture. Umpqua has "stores" throughout Oregon, Washington, Nevada, Idaho, and California. The bank has grown over the years, yet maintains its emphasis on customer service. The bank has been publicized for its service, and executives from other banks will even visit Umpqua to learn about its service-oriented culture.

Umpqua stores feature interactive Discovery Walls, Ritz-Carlton-style concierge desks, and digital cafes with their own brand of coffee. Each store has a phone for customers that rings directly into their CEO's office. He notes that 99% of these calls are to thank him for having a particular banker they work with.[3]

---

3. Lisa Joyce, "Umpqua Bank's New 'Human+Digital' Strategy: A Banker In Every Pocket," 2017, https://thefinancialbrand.com/68810/umpqua-bank-bff-mobile-banking-app/ (accessed February 23, 2018).

Progressive banks talk about "the customer experience." These banks realize that building relationships with customers is paramount and often leads to cross-sales and referrals.

Blunder Bank

At Blunder Bank, the senior management is operations-driven. They are generally opposed to change, using the stale rationale of, "We've always done it this way." When employees make mistakes, they are punished. Service is mediocre at best.

Better Bank

At Better Bank, management constantly reinforces the importance of stellar service. Decisions, policies, and new services are all made with the customer in mind. When mistakes are made, employees are encouraged to use a service recovery approach. Employees are also encouraged to think outside the box when a problem arises rather than to adhere blindly to policy in every situation.

Coaching Tip

During team meetings, emphasize and reinforce the importance of the bank having a service-centric culture. Share examples of stellar service provided by team members.

Questions for Reflection

1. Do your bank's decisions keep the customer at the forefront?

2. Are managers and employees recognized for stellar service?

3. Is the bank open to change that will positively impact service in the long run?

Notes

Chapter 6

Service Recovery

Given the volume of transactions a bank processes, there will be errors made that affect customers.

How a bank handles service errors can mean the difference between a customer closing an account versus strengthening the relationship.

Banks that employ a "service recovery" philosophy understand that by resolving problems quickly and professionally, customers will likely forget about the initial problem. Banks with a service-centric culture react promptly when customer problems are brought to their attention. These banks make it a priority to take care of the customer who has a problem caused by the bank.

One of the first strategies to use, whether the customer is in a branch, on the phone, or emailing the bank, is to use de-escalation techniques to lessen the customer's anger. The following are some examples of de-escalation techniques that can be employed:

- Apologizing
- "Shifting into Neutral"
- Letting the Customer Vent
- Active Listening

A sincere apology will go a long way toward demonstrating empathy and diffusing a customer's anger. It is hard for most customers to stay angry when they hear a sincere apology such as, "I am so sorry that you did not receive your statement this month. I will take care of that so that it does not happen again." A statement such as this also illustrates that you are taking ownership of the problem. Compare this with the deflecting response of, “I have nothing to do with that. You have to call our Operations Center.” Or, some employees, because they personally did not cause the problem, will not apologize.

When customers are upset because of a problem, “shifting into neutral” and letting the customer vent will help de-escalate the situation. By shifting into neutral, employees remain calm, do not become defensive, and do not match the tone of the customer’s voice. Letting the customer vent a little will also allow the customer to have their say. The Anger Pyramid below illustrates that we should first let the customer vent. Then, when the customer reaches the top of the pyramid, that is when we can use

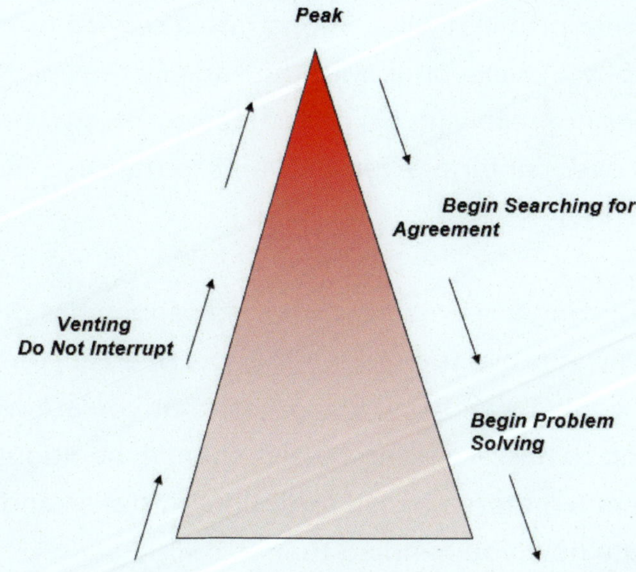

active listening skills to begin to problem solve. Jumping in too early can have the effect of escalating the anger.

Active listening can also help de-escalate a situation. Paraphrasing the customer's situation demonstrates that you truly understand the customer's situation. For example, you could say to Mrs. Wilson, "So it sounds like you did not receive a notice that your CD was maturing and you had wanted to add money to it while it was in the maturity stage. Is that correct?" This also minimizes misunderstandings, as it allows the customer to correct any details you may have missed regarding their problem.

When possible, going above and beyond to resolve a customer problem will demonstrate a service recovery philosophy. For example, with the earlier example of the customer not receiving his or her statement, you could offer to overnight it or even deliver it to the customer's home.

Employing a service recovery philosophy has proven to actually improve the relationship between customers and the bank. By showing customers that you are willing to own up to mistakes, and resolve them expeditiously, customers will more quickly forget the mistakes and appreciate how you handled them.

Blunder Bank

At Blunder Bank, not only does the bank make more than its share of mistakes, but when customers bring them to the bank's attention, employees become defensive. This then can escalate the situation with customers remaining angry with the bank (and telling others about their poor experience).

Better Bank

At Better Bank, management has instilled a service culture whereby employees are empowered to resolve customer problems promptly. Employees receive training on handling customer problems, and departments work together to take care of mistakes that impact customers.

Coaching Tip

After a problem has been discovered and resolved, meet with appropriate bank staff to determine the root cause of the problem.

Questions for Reflection

1. Does your bank allow employees to take ownership of customer problems?

2. Are managers and employees trained on how to work with customers who are upset because of mistakes the bank has made?

3. Do branches and departments work collaboratively to resolve customer problems?

Notes

Chapter 7

Borrow from Other Industries

In general, the banking industry tends to be conservative and does not always think out of the box for ways to be more customer-centric. In fact, it is an industry where those with less formal education than in other industries can rise to higher levels of management. It can also be an industry that has employees who have rarely, or sometimes never, worked in other industries.

Banks would do well to borrow best customer service practices from other industries. For example, much has been written about how fanatical Walt Disney was about customer service.

Today, long after his passing in 1966, any of the Disney Parks still carry his message about service forward. Below are principles that the Disney organization follows.[4]

1. The competition is anyone the customer compares you with.

2. Pay fantastic attention to detail.

3. Everyone walks the talk.

4. Everything walks the talk.

5. Customers are best heard through many ears.

6. Reward, recognize, and celebrate.

Banks can apply the Disney principles to enhance their customer service.

---

4. Connellan, Tom. *Inside The Magic Kingdom: Seven Keys to Disney's Success.* Austin, Bard Press, 2012.

— "The competition is anyone the customer compares you with."

Although in many industries, customer service is mediocre or worse, there are still some customer service stars out there. Remember that your customers may run into these stars and compare you to them. One such star was Ray Porto, who owned and worked at a gas station in Connecticut for over 70 years! Ray was especially known for telling his customers after pumping their gas, to, "Have a sparkling day!" This signature statement along with a positive, friendly, attitude resulted in customers lining up to get gas from Ray over the years. Ray's positive attitude was probably also a factor in his working until he was 92. Those customers smitten with Ray, who then head to or call their bank, may compare the service they had received from Ray with that provided by the bank's staff.

— "Pay fantastic attention to detail."

Banks need to recognize that attention to detail, especially in an industry where they are holding people's money, is critical. Progressive banks realize this and stress to employees the importance of being detail-oriented. Those that do send the message that they are careful and concerned about doing things right the first time. Conversely, inattention to detail can impede a bank's customer service and send a very different, and negative, message.

— "Everyone walks the talk."

Customer-centric banks realize that everyone with whom a customer comes in contact represents the bank. Whether it is a Universal Banker, a call center representative, or a courier, every bank employee has an opportunity to make an impression on customers in a "moment of truth." Senior leaders of a bank would be wise to call their bank from time to time so they can see what their customer experiences, which sometimes is a seemingly endless list of voice-mail options.

— "Everything walks the talk."

Everything about a bank needs to be viewed through a customer's eyes. Below is a list of some of the "everything" that banks must not forget.

- Branch parking lots
- The "look" of the branches (both from the outside and from the lobby)
- The ease of finding information on the bank's website

- Marketing materials
- Social media posts
- How bank employees are dressed and groomed
- The bank's phone system
- Advertising campaigns
- Bank account statements
- Online banking

The above represents a partial list of things that can send a message about how service-oriented a bank is.

— "Customers are best heard through many ears."

Banks would do well to provide multiple options for customers to offer suggestions. Traditional ways of getting customer input has been through customer surveys or focus groups. Don't forget to check with customer-facing staff and your call center about comments they are hearing from customers. These comments may represent patterns that need immediate attention. Also, impromptu calls to customers from the president or a member of senior management are other ways of reaching out.

— "Reward, recognize and celebrate."

To reinforce a culture of service excellence, instances of outstanding service need to, at the very least, be recognized. Even better is to reward and celebrate them. Bank employees will appreciate that their stellar service has been noticed by management.

Banks can also borrow from the hospitality industry, as Ritz-Carlton has long been a leader in providing outstanding service to their guests. Banks who consider their customers "guests" are more likely to create memorable experiences.

Retailers, such as Nordstrom's and Chick-Fil-A, are also known for great service. In fact, more banks are hiring staff with a retail background, being less concerned that they have previous banking experience. These banks appreciate the terrific service that employees from certain retailers provide, and believe they can train these employees so they excel in the banking industry.

Blunder Bank

At Blunder Bank, senior management refuses to consider best practices from other industries. Instead, the bank remains averse to change and not receptive to ways of enhancing their internal and external service. The bank has a 1980's suggestion box in its main office (which would be of more value as a bird feeder) where they look for customers and employees to offer suggestions.

Better Bank

At Better Bank, senior management looks to implement proven customer service practices from different industries in an effort to improve service. In fact, certain staff will "shop" other retailers to learn about practices that can be utilized by the bank. The bank also has a customer experience committee comprised of employees from different departments.

Coaching Tip

At staff meetings, ask the team for examples of great service they have experienced from other industries. Determine whether any of these practices can be implemented at the bank.

Questions for Reflection

1. How often does your bank hire employees from other industries who can bring a fresh service perspective?

2. Does your bank work to continuously improve its service, and consider practices from other industries?

3. How would you rate your bank's service using the 6 principles from Disney discussed in this chapter?

Notes

Chapter 8

Utilize Mystery Shopping

Our observations from working with many banking clients indicate that those banks who do not utilize mystery shopping tend to be less service-oriented.

Mystery shopping can provide an impartial assessment of the service provided by your customer-facing staff.

Progressive banks use the data collected from mystery shops in a developmental, not punitive, way. Managers can use the shops to coach to areas that employees can improve upon. Managers can also recognize those employees who excelled on their shops. Shop results can also uncover patterns that might point out system or procedural bottlenecks.

Some banks utilize their own customers as shoppers. While this can provide some data, often the "halo" effect kicks in and because these customers usually like the bank, the information they are providing is more positive and not impartial. Other banks will use newer back office staff unknown to the branches to conduct shops.

When using a third party vendor to conduct your mystery shopping, be sure that they don't use a cookie cutter approach, whereby all of the financial institutions they shop are assessed on the exact same criteria. Any reputable vendor should be able to customize the shop forms so that they align with your bank's service standards, culture, and work environment. Look to a vendor to provide you with reports by branch, region, and bankwide. Also, be sure that your branches are phone shopped.

Be sure to have your call center shopped. If possible, you can also gather revealing data by having your back office departments shopped, although this can be more challenging to pull off.

Also consider targeted shops. These shops can be conducted after launching a new product or service, opening a new branch, or after a systems conversion.

On the next few pages are sample teller, platform, and call center shop forms. Be sure not to over-shop, where branches are, for example, shopped every week.

Mystery Shopper Survey – Teller

Branch: **Date:** **Time:**

Employee Name:

Shopper Initials:

Branch Appearance	Y	N	N/A
1. Was the outside signage clear and visible?			
2. Were the exterior grounds neat and clean?			
3. Was the ATM area neat and clean?			
4. Was the lobby clean and uncluttered?			
5. Was promotional signage visible?			

Greeting Skills	Y	N	N/A
6. Did the employee offer a sincere friendly greeting or opening remark?			
7. Did the employee smile?			
8. Was the employee's name tag visible?			

Comments:

____

____

____

____

____

____

____

____

Customer Service	Y	N	N/A
9. Was the employee dressed professionally?			
10. Was the employee attentive?			
11. Was the employee helpful?			
12. Did the employee conduct him/herself professionally?			
13. Did the employee process the transaction efficiently?			
14. Did the employee process the transaction correctly?			
15. Did the employee attempt to cross-sell?			
16. Did the employee conclude the transaction with a standard closing?			

Comments:

____

____

____

____

____

____

____

____

____

____

____

Mystery Shopper Survey – Telephone

Branch: **Date:** **Time:**

Employee Name:

Shopper:

Service Standard	Y	N	N/A
1. Call answered within three rings			
2. Employee answered pleasantly saying "Thank you for calling ________" or "Good morning/afternoon, ________"			
3. Employee asked, "How may I help you?"			
4. Employee was pleasant			
5. Employee obtained person's name and used it at least once during the conversation			
6. Employee was helpful			
7. Employee was able to to suggest appropriate product/service			
8. If caller had a problem, employee took ownership of it and worked towards solution			
9. If appropriate, employee gave phone # and name of employee being transferred to			
10. Employee concluded call with a standard closing such as "Have a great day"			

Type of transaction/inquiry performed (e.g., inquired about CD rates, asked about a home equity loan):

____

____

Comments:

____

____

____

Mystery Shopper Survey – Platform

Branch: **Date:** **Time:**

Employee Name:

Shopper:

Service Standard	Y	N	N/A
1. Employee smiled and used standard greeting such as "Good Morning"			
2. Employee made a positive first impression with a neat and clean look			
3. Employee made eye contact			
4. Employee introduced him/herself			
5. Employee obtained customer's name			
6. Employee stood and directed customer to a seat			
7. Employee was able to answer questions about products and services			
8. If appropriate, employee picked up on a cross-sell cue			
9. Customer was asked if there is anything else you can help them with			
10. Customer was given the employee's business card			
11. Customer was thanked with a standard greeting such as, "Have a great day"			

Type of transaction/inquiry performed (e.g., inquired about IRA, asked about a home equity loan):

____

____

Comments:

____

____

Blunder Bank

At Blunder Bank, the senior management feels their service is sufficient and there is no need to shop the bank. In addition, they don't want to spend money on an outside firm providing the mystery shops. Not surprisingly, the bank receives ongoing complaints from customers that reveal patterns of poor service.

Better Bank

At Better Bank, the senior management values mystery shopping. Management looks for patterns among shop data collected, so as to find ways to enhance their service. Managers use the shop results developmentally, to coach staff on ways to improve their service provided. They also recognize their top performers.

Coaching Tip

Managers should not only address poor shops, but also excellent shops. Praise employees whose shop scores are high and be specific with your feedback. For example, if the shopper noted that the employee demonstrated strong product knowledge, let the employee know that, as opposed to simply saying, "Good job with your June shop."

Questions for Reflection

1. When was the last time your bank was shopped?

2. Do you use your shop results in a constructive way?

3. Do you look at your shop data with an eye toward bankwide changes to enhance your service?

Notes

Chapter 9

Train, Re-Train, and Train Again

Just as banks are required to provide compliance training periodically (e.g., Bank Secrecy Act), progressive banks treat customer service the same way and provide training on it regularly.

As with any training you provide, follow principles of adult learning to ensure that your programs are engaging, relevant, and skills-based. Avoid lectures and PowerPoint.

The following are some of the topics to include in a bank's customer service training program:

- Interpersonal Communication Skills
- Handling Challenging Customers
- Problem Solving
- Service Recovery
- Exceeding Customer Expectations
- Wowing the Customer

Also, include and reinforce your bank's service standards in the training.

Demonstrate the link between stellar service and sales during the training. Banks that provide outstanding service can more easily cross-sell other products and services to existing customers.

Consider whether to utilize your internal training department to facilitate customer service training or to bring in a vendor. An internal person will be more familiar with your products and services, while a consultant provides perspectives gained from working with other organizations.

Remember that all of your customer training does not need to be classroom based. Webinars, podcasts, online training, and blended learning solutions can also be effective.

Follow-up on-the-job training can ensure that customer service remains top-of-mind among employees. Cross-train your staff so that they acquire additional knowledge and skills that enable them to provide stellar service. Use written procedures and job aids as reminders of key concepts. Utilize the "Playscript" format shown on the following pages to ensure that your procedures are easy to follow.

Playscript Format for Writing Procedures or Instructions

Procedure Writing

Documenting procedures involves the write-up that reflects a certain system. A written procedure clearly spells out how an activity flows from one work group to the next, from start to finish. The procedure explains the way people who run the system proceed to do their work. One style of writing procedures uses the Playscript format. The procedure below is first shown in a long-winded, narrative style, then in the Playscript style.

Version A

The referenced procedure places the responsibility upon the requesting department to completely justify the necessity for additional equipment and/or facilities. In order to assist the requesting departments, a form, "Facilities Request," No. 347, has been made available to all departments, and if this form is completely filled out it will not only comply with Standard Practice Instruction #74, but will greatly facilitate the review and, in case of need, the acquisition of the required items. At the present time, many requests are coming to Facilities Engineering by e-mail, verbally, and in other forms that are either incomplete or inaccurate. A careful use of Form 347 will react to the benefit of both the requester and to the Company. As a further aid, if the requester will send two copies of Form 347 to Facilities Engineering, one copy will be returned with the assigned job number and preliminary action indicated which will give the requester quickly a status of his or her request, and also will serve as a ready reference file.

Version B

Subject: Requesting Assistance from Facilities	
Action by	Action
Requester	1. Complete form 347, "Facilities Request" in three copies.
	2. Sends 2 copies to Facilities Engineering.
Facilities engineering	3. Assigns job number to both copies of the request, indicating when preliminary action will be taken.
	4. Returns one copy of form 347 to Requester.
Requester	5. In case of any inquiry, refers to job number of request.
Facilities engineering	6. Reviews all requests.
	7. Determines relative facility needs of various departments.
	8. Allocates available funds in accordance with such needs.

Below is another example of a Playscript procedure.

Procedure Name:	Stop Payments
Date Issued:	7/9/2018
Issued By:	Retail Administration
Date Revised	
Revised by:	

STOP PAYMENTS

Action By:	Action:
Branch Representative	1. Receive the stop payment request from the customer. 2. Perform a checking account history inquiry on the DeskTop system to determine if check has already been paid. Inform the customer and ask if there is anything else that you can help them with. 3. If the check has not been paid, pull up the Stop Payment Order transaction on the DeskTop system and enter the following information obtained from the customer: (a) Name of Payee on check to be stopped (b) Reason for stop payment (c) Check Number (d) Date of check (e) Amount of check (f) Account number (g) Duplicate issues

Action By:	Action:
Branch Representative	4. Inform the customer that their account will be charged $25 for the stop payments, unless their account is one where this fee can be waived. 5. Print out the stop payment form and have the customer verify all the information for accuracy, then have them sign the stop payment form. 6. Make a copy of the stop payment form and give it to the customer. 7. Send the original to the Operations Department. 8. Stop Payment Orders are active for six months or until the item is returned unpaid.

Don't forget to provide training for managers and supervisors focused on Coaching for Service Excellence. This training will reinforce a bank's service-centric culture. Be sure that your call center receives periodic training.

Also provide customer service training to your bank's back office staff. These employees are sometimes forgotten when it comes to training, yet their role in providing outstanding internal service is critical to a bank's success. Be sure that this training is customized so that the curriculum addresses opportunities and challenges specific to the bank's back office.

Blunder Bank

At Blunder Bank, new employees sit through a lecture-based, PowerPoint training session on customer service that also includes a dated "talking-head" video. Follow-up training on the topic is non-existent, unless there are service problems, in which case any follow-up training is viewed as punitive.

Better Bank

At Better Bank, customer service is emphasized from Day One, in the bank's orientation and onboarding program. Engaging customer service training is provided regularly. This training is interactive and skills-based, and includes both customer-facing and non-customer-facing staff.

Coaching Tip

Keep in mind that roughly three-quarters of employees are visual learners. Therefore, ensure that your classroom training utilizes methodologies where employees can "see" a concept. Also, with on-the-job training, ensure that employees are "showing" other employees, instead of only "telling" them.

Questions for Reflection

1. Does your customer service training align and reinforce the bank's service standards?

2. Does the bank also offer service training for back office staff?

3. Are managers and supervisors provided with customer service training so that they can coach to it with their staff?

Notes

Chapter 10

Internal Service and Teamwork

Banks with a culture of outstanding service realize that their internal service and teamwork is just as important as their external service.

For back office staff, having documented procedures

can lessen errors made which impact service to customers. Ensure that these procedures are kept current and that new back office staff are trained on them.

Implement a system of shadowing and partnership where back office staff spend time in a branch so that they better recognize the urgency of problem solving and responding to customers. Conversely, have branch and other customer-facing staff spend time in the back office so they appreciate the multiple priorities and challenges back office staff face.

With your internal recognition programs on customer service, be sure that all employees are included, not just customer-facing employees. This sends a message that the bank values internal service just as much as external service.

Tied into internal service is teamwork. John Maxwell notes the 17 Qualities of team players.[5]

1. Adaptable: If You Won't Change for the Team, the Team May Change You

---

5. Maxwell, John C. *The 17 Essential Qualities of a Team Player: Becoming the Kind of Person Every Team Wants*. Nashville, Thomas Nelson, Inc., 2002.

2. Collaborative: Working Together Precedes Winning Together
3. Committed: There are no Halfhearted Champions
4. Communicative: A Team is Many Voices with a Single Heart
5. Competent: If You Can't, Your Team Won't
6. Dependable: Teams Go to Go-To Players
7. Disciplined: Where There's a Will, There's a Win
8. Enlarging: Adding Value to Teammates is Invaluable
9. Enthusiastic: Your Heart is the Source of Energy for the Team
10. Intentional: Make Every Action Count
11. Mission Conscious: The Big Picture is Coming in Loud and Clear
12. Prepared: Preparation Can Mean the Difference Between Winning and Losing
13. Relational: If You Get Along, Others will Go Along
14. Self-Improving: To Improve the Team, Improve Yourself
15. Selfless: There is no "I" in Team

16. Solution Oriented: Make a Resolution to Find the Solution

17. Tenacious: Never, Never, Never Quit

Managers can foster teamwork in a variety of ways. Publicizing when employees go above and beyond shares examples of teamwork and stellar internal service. Managers can also have occasional breakfasts and lunches for their department or branch, where employees can get to better know their co-workers. Getting involved in bank-sponsored community events also forges teamwork and improved working relationships, leading to enhanced internal service. Formal team-building sessions can also strengthen the bonds between employees who are providing service to each other.

Blunder Bank

At Blunder Bank, the back office is viewed as a haven for individuals who are not service-oriented or team players. Turnover is high and there is an adversarial relationship

between back office and customer-facing staff, which affects the bank's internal service and, ultimately, the service provided to customers.

Better Bank

At Better Bank, management demonstrates through its actions how important internal service and teamwork are. Examples of stellar internal service are publicized and recognized. The bank also hires employees for back office positions who have experience working directly with customers, which improves the internal service and creates a more collaborative relationship between back office employees and customer-facing employees.

Coaching Tip

Explaining the reasons behind certain bank policies and procedures (e.g., regulatory), can help ensure compliance, and improve internal service.

Questions for Reflection

1. Do you have back office staff who have some experience on the front line with customers?

2. Do you recognize examples of outstanding internal service?

3. Do you provide cross-exposure to employees so that customer-facing staff spend time in the back office, and vice versa?

Notes

Chapter 11

Utilize a Universal Banker Approach Within Your Branches

Foot traffic in bank branches has decreased over the years. Research suggests that this will continue to be the case.

In large part because of fewer customers going into branches, many banks employ a Universal Banker approach, whereby all (or almost all) branch staff can handle most platform and teller transactions. If your bank has not already moved to a Universal Banker approach, why haven't you?

While having Universal Bankers reduces expenses since you need fewer employees in each branch, it also can improve the service for customers who go to your branches. For example, if Mrs. Smith has questions about a home equity loan, and your platform staff are with other customers, an employee behind the teller line should be able to help her (rather than having Mrs. Smith waste time sitting until a platform employee is available).

Ensure that your Universal Bankers are trained on both teller and platform functions so that they can provide stellar service by answering all of the customer's questions. Utilize your core system's documentation and bank policies and procedures in your training. Having well trained Universal Bankers also allows you to send an employee from Branch A to Branch B, when Branch B is shorthanded.

When hiring Universal Bankers, also look for individuals who can multi-task and juggle multiple priorities.

Here are 10 questions to consider regarding Universal Banking:

1. Is your bank ready for the cultural change necessary to implement Universal Banking?

2. Has Universal Banking been adequately embraced by the senior leadership?

3. Has the Universal Banking concept been adequately communicated throughout the bank?

4. Have you identified the skills and competencies necessary for Universal Banker success?

5. Have you skill mapped your existing employees to determine if they have the necessary skills for Universal Banker success and to identify where gaps exist?

6. Have you adequately trained hiring managers to recruit candidates that have the necessary skills through appropriate behavioral interviewing?

7. Have you established service standards by which to measure Universal Banker success?

8. Do you have a feedback mechanism in place to measure Universal Banker progress on sales and service?

9. Have you tied learning objectives in Universal Banker training to specific service metrics to ensure that training is effective?

10. Have your employees been adequately trained in all the products and services provided by your bank? Do you provide periodic refreshers to ensure they have adequate knowledge?

Bank presidents who think they can snap their fingers and immediately convert a traditional branch approach to a Universal Banker approach are sadly mistaken. Adequate role definition and training must be part of this change.

Keep in mind that you don't necessarily need to use "Universal Banker" as the title for your branch staff. Some banks refer to them as "customer service associates," "customer relationship bankers," or "customer service representatives."

Blunder Bank

At Blunder Bank, the president, Mr. Clueless, heard about Universal Banking while at a conference. He came back and immediately implemented Universal Banking in all of the bank's branches, without providing any training for the staff. The employees were confused, untrained, and service to branch customers suffered.

Better Bank

At Better Bank, a team planned for the bank's transition to Universal Bankers. Management clearly communicated their vision and the new role of branch staff to all employees. Universal Banker's roles were defined, excitement was created, and training was provided.

Coaching Tip

Remember that a switch to Universal Bankers is a change. Like with any change, there will be a learning curve and those who resist the change. Work with employees who are struggling with this change and, if needed, provide them with additional training.

Questions for Reflection

1. Have you considered going to a Universal Banker format? If not, why?

2. Do you provide comprehensive training to your Universal Bankers?

3. Do you recognize the stellar service provided by your Universal Bankers?

Notes

Chapter 12

Make Sure Your Systems are not Impediments to Stellar Service

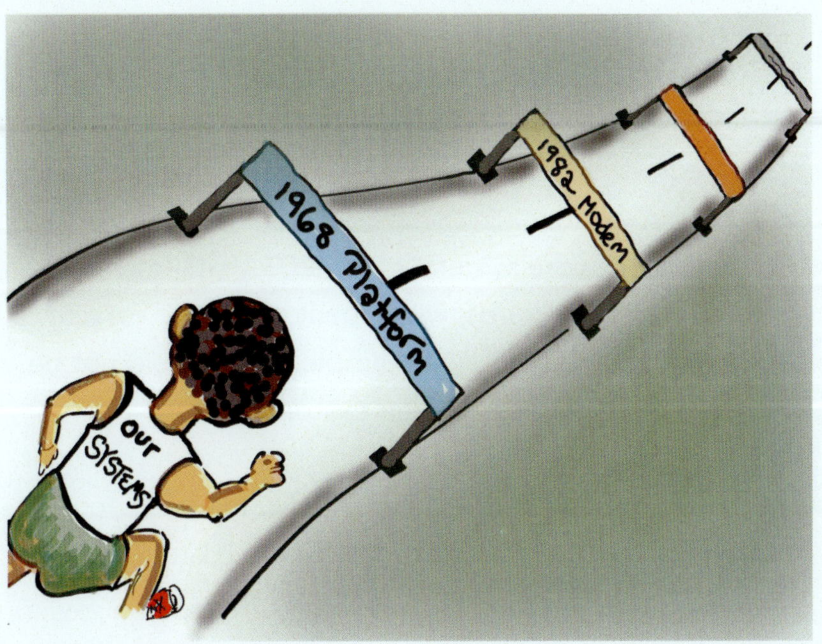

Customer-centric banks have systems that support, not impede, their customers' experiences with them.

Starting with their core system, banks must ensure that their core system provider remains state-of-the-art and not "user-hostile." Often, every 5-7 years, a bank's contract with its core service provider comes up for renewal. Many banks, because of their employees' comfort with the system, will automatically renew, rather than determining whether there is a more state-of-the-art digital system available that enhances the customer experience.

The bank's core system, coupled with its internal systems and procedures, will impact customer service. Take opening accounts, for example. This should not be a cumbersome process for the customer, or the bank employee, where it takes a half hour to open an account. We know of several banks where opening an account is so laborious that branch staff suggest customers or prospective customers set up appointments to do so.

A core system should also be evaluated on the ease of use and intuitiveness of back office, loan, and sales functions as well. Can it support ancillary systems, such as mortgage and loan origination? Does it incorporate the latest compliance and security measures?

With fewer customers coming into the bank, online banking needs to be easy to use. At one bank, the online banking system is so complicated, that branch staff hesitate to bring it up as an option to customers, for fear that the customer will ask for a demonstration by the employees, who will likely struggle with it!

Other internal systems, such as General Ledger, should be reviewed periodically for ways to streamline them.

A bank should also update its policies and procedures, and have them readily accessible for customer-facing employees. As previously noted, procedures using the Playscript format are easier to write and follow, as opposed to ones written as a lengthy paragraph narrative.

Blunder Bank

At Blunder Bank, the same core system has been used for decades. The system is outdated and difficult to use. Customer-facing employees even develop their own "work arounds" so that customers are not inconvenienced by it.

Better Bank

At Better Bank, senior management asks, “How can this enhance the customer experience?” when designing, revamping, or purchasing systems. The bank ensures that employees receive timely training on their systems and maintain up-to-date, easy-to-follow documentation.

Coaching Tip

When working with an employee who is struggling to use a new system, which can impede service to your customers, remember that everyone has their own learning style. It may be that the struggling employee is a visual learner, and needs to spend more time navigating the system to better comprehend it.

Questions for Reflection

1. Do your employees receive timely training on your internal systems?

2. Is there up-to-date documentation for all of your systems?

3. Does your core processing system enhance or impede the customer experience?

Notes

Chapter 13

Is Your Call Center Effective?

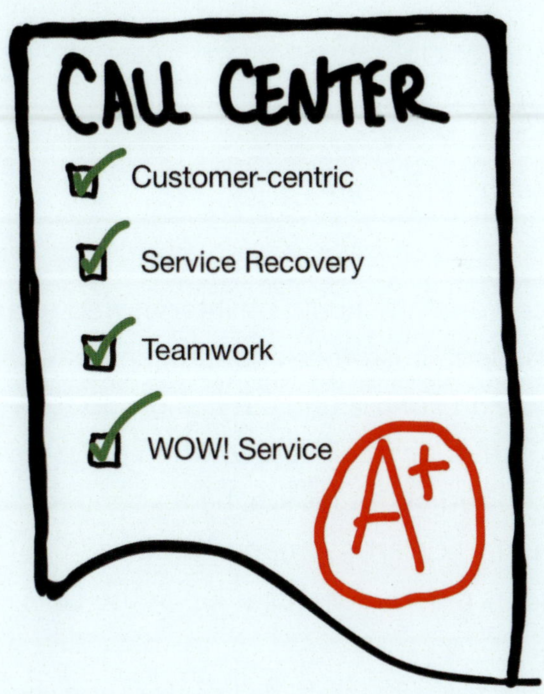

Most banks' views of a cell center fall into one of two categories. The bank may view its call center as a virtual branch, or it may view it as an outpost for employees unsuited to work in a branch.

For a bank to have its call center considered a virtual branch, the following factors must be considered:

- Skills of Call Center Representatives
- Compensation for Call Center Representatives
- Hours of Operation
- System Used
- Training Provided

Call center staff should be interviewed to ensure that they are patient, customer-oriented, and have a pleasant phone voice. In conducting a focus group for one financial institution's call center, when a rep was asked what he disliked about his job, he responded, "Being on the phone!" Clearly, someone dropped the ball in selecting this person for a position in the call center.

To attract quality staff, call center reps should at least be compensated on par with certain branch positions such as platform CSRs or Universal Bankers. Also, incentivize them for opening accounts or cross-selling.

Make sure that your call center is adequately staffed and available to customers throughout the day (and on Saturday). It is important to offer extended hours on weekends, at least. Nothing is more frustrating for customers than waiting in the system's queue for several minutes before you can actually talk to an employee.

Some banks will have positions where the employee splits his or her time between working in a branch and the call center.

Invest in a system for your call center that is customer-friendly and also provides metrics about your calls. Train the call center staff thoroughly on the system, including any enhancements to it.

Beyond customer service training, don't forget your call center staff when it comes to product and sales training. The call center supervisor should also provide ongoing coaching, especially for newer staff.

Identify call center metrics to determine your call center's effectiveness. Metrics such as first call resolution and abandoned calls can tell a bank a lot about how well its call center is doing. Also have your call center mystery shopped.

Blunder Bank

At Blunder Bank, the call center consists of employees who have performed poorly in their roles in other departments or branches of the bank. Consequently, the bank receives many complaints about the call center. The system used is antiquated and poses a problem for both customers and staff.

Better Bank

Better Bank invests in its call center - both in the staff and in their system. The bank views its call center as a virtual branch and has many employees working in it who are lauded by customers. The call center's supervisor acts as a coach and provides rewards and recognition when the call center reaches certain goals.

Coaching Tip

It takes employees with a certain skillset and patience to work in your call center. With call center representatives who are struggling, it may be that it is not a coaching issue and they are just not cut out to work in a call center.

Questions for Reflection

1. Have you ever made a call to your call center posing as a potential customer so you can gain a first-hand experience?

2. Do you periodically benchmark the salaries and commissions of your call center staff?

3. Do you ensure that call center staff are included in Product training, as well as Sales/Service training?

Notes

Chapter 14

Service Over the Phone, via e-mail, by Mail, and Virtually

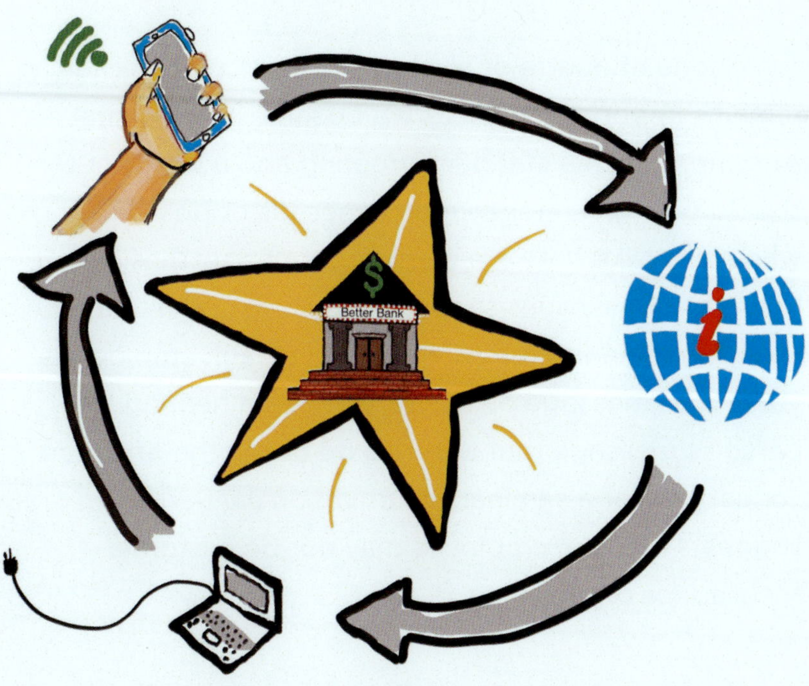

Customer-centric banks recognize that all communication with customers, not just face-to-face, needs to be handled professionally.

For some banks, calls to the bank and access to their

phone system can be an indication that they actually prefer not speaking with customers. Cumbersome phone systems, where customers can get caught in endless loops trying to find a person or department, frustrates customers and demonstrates the institution's lack of concern.

Phone etiquette of all staff, not just customer-facing, remains important, even as we become more digital. Answering with a standard greeting and a pleasant tone should be a given for all employees (as opposed to those who sound like they are coming out of anesthesia!). Voice-mail messages should also sound upbeat, and be kept concise and current. Reaching a bank employee's voice-mail message on January 25th and hearing the person's message that they will be out of the office on January 19th at a seminar, returning on January 22nd, suggests that the employee may not be customer-focused (or organized).

If you are e-mailing a customer, ensure that the tone is positive, and be concise. Be sure to spell-check and proofread your e-mail so that it's not riddled with typos, or inaccurate/incomplete information. Do not write your e-mails as if you are texting a friend!

With any letters you need to mail to customers, follow the same principles noted above for e-mails. Also project a professional look to the letter through proper business formatting. Also be sure to have someone sign the letter. One of our colleagues recently closed out a CD with a bank, and received a letter from the bank signed as "Mail Teller."

When sending out a marketing mailing to customers and prospects, less is more. Fewer mailings will be more impactful. Don't include too much information in one mailing or you may cause a "confusion of abundance" for the recipient.

Also evaluate your account statements. Are they professional looking and easy to follow? Or do they resemble a computer screen dump?

With more customers using a bank's online banking system and its mobile apps, make sure that your systems and apps are intuitive and easy to use. Train your customer-facing staff to provide brief demos of these services to your customers. Also include tutorials on your website. Train your customer-facing employees to use the tutorials so that they can easily demo them with customers.

Blunder Bank

At Blunder Bank, the bank has an antiquated phone system it installed over fifteen years ago. Customers are frustrated when trying to navigate through it. Also, bank statements mailed to customers are confusing and their look hasn't changed in years.

Better Bank

At Better Bank, the bank periodically upgrades its phone system, and provides training on using it (as well as on phone etiquette) to all employees. Mailings to customers are clean and concise. The bank's online banking system is easy to navigate, and staff are prepared to assist customers who bank online or through their mobile devices.

Coaching Tip

If you need an employee to improve their phone etiquette, consider having the employee shadow an employee with very good phone etiquette. Be mindful that our younger generations - Millennials and Gen Z - do not use the phone as much as older generations and may not be aware of some of the basics of telephone etiquette.

Questions for Reflection

1. When was the last time you evaluated your phone system?

2. Do you provide training to bank staff on phone etiquette and e-mail communication?

3. Are your online banking system and mobile apps easy to navigate?

Notes

Chapter 15

Remove Bad Fits and Bad Apples

It is inevitable that some bank employees will not work out and will need to be managed out. These employees may have been poor hires who do not have the knowledge and skillset needed to properly represent your financial institution. However, this should be a last resort, and before you get to this point, work with the employee so they have every opportunity to improve.

Employees struggling in any of these areas below will adversely impact the bank's level of service:

- Disorganized
- Resists Change
- Unable to Master Your Systems
- Not a Team Player
- Lack of Product Knowledge
- Poor Communicator
- Bad Attitude
- Lack of Emotional Intelligence

With struggling employees, determine whether the employee can't do it, or won't do it.

With employees who can't do it, coaching, re-training or job shadowing may improve their skillset. Managers need to hold employees accountable for making improvements.

With employees who won't do it, you have bigger problems. While you should still attempt to coach the employee for improved performance, this scenario often suggests an employee who is not a team player, has a poor attitude, or who is lazy. When this is the case, start your bank's progressive discipline process, so that if the employee does not change and show improvement, you can terminate them (consulting with Human Resources).

When documentation becomes necessary, also consult with your HR area. If termination becomes necessary, hande it respectfully, since you don't want a disgruntled employee to badmouth the bank within your community. For higher level employees, consider offering them outplacement services.

Blunder Bank

At Blunder Bank, there are several poor hires who do not have the requisite skills. These employees provide poor service to both external and internal customers. However, these employees are allowed to continue to provide poor service, and so the employees stay, yet are unproductive and an impediment to stellar service.

Better Bank

At Better Bank, when a poor hire is made, or an employee is struggling, these employees are made aware of their shortcomings. Managers hold these employees accountable and provide avenues such as coaching and training to help them improve. When necessary, the bank may need to terminate the employee so that they do not negatively impact service to customers and co-workers. When this is the case, the process is handled properly, with guidance from Human Resources.

Coaching Tip

Determine the root cause as to why an employee is struggling. Be sure that you are providing regular feedback so that the employee is aware of deficiencies and given an opportunity to improve.

Questions for Reflection

1. Do you determine whether an underperforming employee is in the can't do or won't do category?

2. Do your managers hold employees accountable for quality service to customers and co-workers?

3. Do you manage out employees who are not a fit or are bad apples?

Notes

Chapter 16

Look to Continuously Innovate

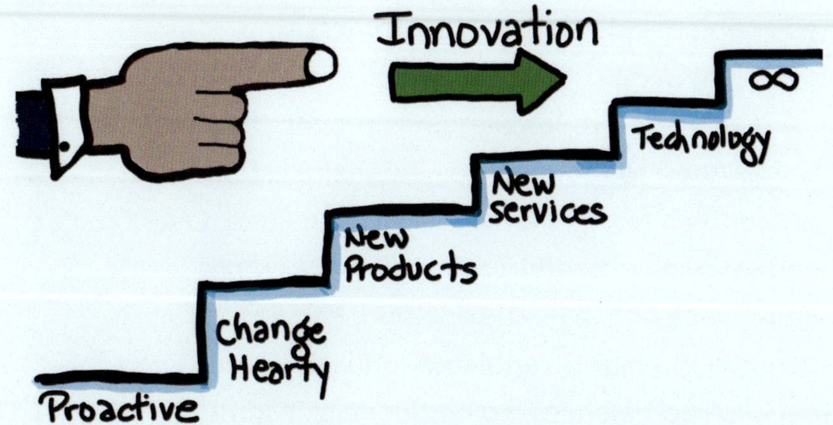

Progressive financial institutions recognize the need to continuously innovate in order to serve customers even better. Your marketing department should be leading the way with innovation. Yet we sometimes see marketing departments that are transactional, and not creative. These departments focus on traditional marketing (brochures, websites, mailings), but do not think out of the box. Learn from what your competitors are doing, and from service providers in different industries. Shop other financial institutions to look for practices that can be implemented at your bank. Also be on the lookout for products and services that others are offering that you can consider for your customers.

Connected to innovation is process improvement. Banks need to regularly review their systems and procedures to ensure they are streamlined. Over time, certain bank procedures can become cumbersome for employees and, by extrapolation, customers. While banking is a highly regulated industry, with a need for checks and balances, some financial institutions take this to an excessive degree. For example, because of a one-time incident, the bank may institute a cumbersome procedure that is unnecessary. Look to see how these procedures can be simplified.

Also connected to innovation is strategic planning. A bank's senior leaders will often meet once a year to develop their strategic plan. That is not enough! Strategic planning should be a part of the senior team's regular meetings. Progressive banks will also strategize with other levels of management for innovative ideas.

The kryptonite for innovation is resistance to change. If there is one constant in every organization today, including banks, it is change. New products, regulations, systems, and technology are just some of the examples of changes in the industry. Beware of the "but we've always done it that way" mindset. It can emanate from a bank's board and/or its senior management. Once changes are made, they can be met with resistance by lower level managers and staff. Change management training, where dealing with resistance is addressed, can help a bank deal with change.

Blunder Bank

At Blunder Bank, the organization is stuck with the mindset that, "If it's not broken, don't fix it." As a result, the bank rarely provides new products and services for customers. The bank's marketing department is transactional in nature, and along with its senior leaders, see no need to innovate. In fact, innovation or change of any sort is frowned upon.

Better Bank

At Better Bank, senior management looks for ways to be creative and also to continuously improve the way they do business. This mindset permeates throughout the bank, as the marketing department holds periodic focus groups of managers and employees (and customers) to brainstorm on ways to enhance the customer experience.

Coaching Tip

Don't forget when coaching employees to ask them for suggestions on how a process or procedure might be simplified, especially when it impacts the customer experience.

Questions for Reflection

1. Do you periodically look at your systems and procedures to seek opportunities to streamline them?

2. Does your senior team engage in regular strategic planning (not just once a year going off-site for two days!)?

3. Is your marketing department innovative and leading the organization in developing new ideas?

Notes

Chapter 17

Customer Service Derailers

While we've noted ways for banks to improve their service, these eight items will derail a bank from its outstanding customer service delivery goals.

1. Overly Conservative Board of Directors - It is recognized that the banking industry, by nature, is conservative. However, some banks have overly conservative board members who are resistant to innovative products, services, systems, and technology that will enhance the customer service. Often, the board is comprised of mostly white males in their 60's or older, who may be set in their ways. A bank can improve the creativity and innovation of its board by ensuring its members are younger and more diverse. While it's understandable to have an attorney and an accountant on your board, you should also have marketing and technology professionals.

2. A Senior Management Team Set in its Ways - We know that some banks have senior leaders who have climbed the corporate ladder and may not have worked outside of the banking industry. The more innovative bank senior management teams include individuals who have worked in different industries, who come with ideas and best customer service practices from outside of banking. A bank's president needs to discourage groupthink, and ensure that out-of-the-box thinking is encouraged and occurring among his or her senior leaders.

3. An Operations-Driven Culture - Hearing a bank brag about how they are operations-focused is often code for their not being sales and service focused. While the nature of banking requires controls, progressive banks create a customer-oriented culture where employees are empowered when working with customers. Not having bankwide service standards often equates to the bank not being progressive with its service practices.

4. Poor Hires - Hiring the least expensive outside candidate for open positions is short sighted. Promotions based mostly on longevity with the bank is also generally a poor hiring practice. Especially for customer-facing positions, seek enthusiastic candidates who recognize the importance of the bank's customers. Some banks will include testing as part of their pre-employment practices. Many of these tests look only at basic math and vocabulary skills. Ensure that HR and hiring managers are asking behavioral interview questions to determine how candidates have worked with customers in the past. Also consider candidates with non-banking retail experience.

5. Managers Who Don't Hold Employees Accountable - As we've discussed, a key to stellar service are the managers overseeing the employees who provide

the service. Managers who avoid conflict and overlook poor service will lose credibility. These managers need to hold employees accountable for stellar service and, when appropriate, recognize and reward them for exceeding customer expectations. Managers of back office staff should also hold their employees accountable for outstanding internal service and, when appropriate, recognize and reward them for stellar internal service.

6. Lack of and/or Poor Training - Banks who do not invest in their employees will pay for this in the long run. As a heavily regulated industry, all banks offer mandatory compliance training. Banks should also offer mandatory and regular customer service training, along with other topics related to service such as Communication, Emotional Intelligence, Project Management, and Change Management.

7. Averse to Change - Often by walking into a bank's branch, one can discern how open the bank is to change. If the décor and appearance look like it's a flashback to the '90's, rest assured that the bank is usually not progressive and open to change. The "we've always done it this way" mentality also signals a bank that resists change and will not be open to cutting-edge products or technology.

8. Outdated Systems – Whether it's the bank's core processing system, phone system, or even its equipment, continuing to use outdated systems impedes both internal and external service. Banks unwilling to invest in state-of-the-art systems miss out on ways to enhance their customer experience.

Notes

Chapter 18

Examples of WOW Service

Those financial institutions that create a service culture are more likely to have employees who will demonstrate WOW service. Recognizing that not every interaction with customers affords a chance to demonstrate WOW service, employees who get it look for situations where they can wow the customer.

WOW service is when an employee goes above and beyond and provides a memorable experience for the customer. The experience often results in the customer telling others about it.

Here are some examples of WOW service.

During the middle of winter, at 5:45, just before the branch was closing at 6 p.m., a customer left the branch and found her car battery dead. She called AAA and then went back into the branch to let them know that her car battery was dead, AAA would be coming, and she would need to wait in her car in the bank parking lot after the bank closed. Overhearing this customer's story, the assistant branch manager, Jane, told the customer to wait in the branch lobby, offered her coffee, and said that she could wait inside until AAA arrived. Even though the branch closed to the public at 6 p.m., Jane did not want the woman waiting in a cold car during the middle of winter. As you can imagine, the customer was deeply appreciative of Jane's kindness and WOW service.

During tax season, a customer, on very short notice, called one of the branches and mentioned he needed copies of his bank statements for his accountant. Sensing the stress level of this customer, Pat, a Universal Banker, told the customer he would print them out and drive to the customer's house, and drop them off. The customer was relieved and has been telling everyone about the great service this bank, and Pat, in particular, provided.

A customer contacted the bank's call center, frustrated because she was not easily able to navigate the bank's online banking system. Maria, the call center representative, could sense the frustration in the customer's voice. Noticing that the customer lived down the street from the bank's main office, Maria asked the customer if she might be available to stop by the branch at noon, where Maria would meet her and walk her through the online system. Maria gave up her lunch period and worked with the customer on a computer in the main office. The customer was thrilled to now have a better understanding of how to conduct transactions online. The next day the customer came back to the main office with a plate of homemade cookies for Maria.

A newly married couple was buying their first house and considering getting a mortgage with the bank where they have their checking accounts. The couple, admittedly, was not aware of the process of obtaining a mortgage. Gary, one of the bank's mortgage originators, took the time to write a checklist of things the couple needed to do. Deeply appreciative of Gary taking the time not only to provide the checklist but also to walk through the steps in detail, the couple decided to obtain their mortgage through Gary and his bank. They have since referred others seeking a mortgage to Gary.

A family was excited to be leaving for vacation the next day. While packing at 5:30 the night before leaving, that excitement waned when the husband revealed he had lost his ATM card. The man called the bank, reaching a call center representative. Hearing the man's plight, Sarah, the call center representative, asked how far away the customer lived from any of the bank's branches. The customer responded that he was just ten minutes away from the bank's downtown branch. With the customer still on the line, Sarah called the assistant branch manager of the bank's downtown branch and explained the customer's dilemma. Although the bank was closing in ten minutes, the assistant branch manager asked the customer if he was able to come to the branch, where she could make a replacement ATM card for him. The customer was thrilled and went to the branch to obtain a replacement ATM card. The teamwork demonstrated by the call center representative and the assistant branch manager so impressed the customer that when he returned from vacation, he moved the money from a CD that was maturing with another bank to this bank.

Mrs. Watson, an older customer, has a portfolio with the bank's Investment Advisor, Jim. The account is joint with her daughter, who now lives out of state. Mrs. Watson left a voice-mail message for Jim, explaining that her daughter would be visiting for the weekend, and she could not find her most recent statement. The Investment Advisor, Jim, was away on vacation, but occasionally checked his voice-mail messages. When he heard Mrs. Watson's message, he immediately called his colleague, Denise, and asked if she could overnight the statement to Mrs. Watson. Jim also called Mrs. Watson to let her know that the statement would be there the next morning when her daughter would be with her. Mrs. Watson was thrilled with Jim's prompt response, and when she told her daughter about it, her daughter decided to move more money from another account to Jim.

Conclusion

As a former banker who has consulted with hundreds of banks, I have seen the good, the bad, and the ugly regarding customer service.

The good news is that banking is not rocket science, and with a progressive senior leadership team, a bank's service can be improved.

Following the practices outlined in this book can serve to enhance your bank's commitment to stellar service. Remember the adage, "You never get a second chance to make a good first impression."